Discovery™

I Am a
PENGUIN

Level 1

Written by Lori C. Froeb

PRE-LEVEL 1: ASPIRING READERS

 LEVEL 1: EARLY READERS

- Basic factual texts with familiar themes and content
- Concepts in text are reinforced by photos
- Includes glossary to reinforce reading comprehension
- Phonic regularity
- Simple sentence structure and repeated sentence patterns
- Easy vocabulary familiar to kindergarteners and first graders

 LEVEL 2: DEVELOPING READERS

 LEVEL 3: ENGAGED READERS

 LEVEL 4: FLUENT READERS

Silver Dolphin Books
An imprint of Printers Row Publishing Group
A division of Readerlink Distribution Services, LLC
10350 Barnes Canyon Road, Suite 100, San Diego, CA 92121
www.silverdolphinbooks.com

ISBN: 978-1-64517-232-1
Manufactured, printed, and assembled in Rawang, Selangor, Malaysia.
First printing, May 2020. THP/05/20
24 23 22 21 20 1 2 3 4 5

Hi there! I am a penguin.
This is my family.
We are emperor penguins.

There are around eighteen **species** of penguins. Emperor penguins are the largest species.

I am a male emperor penguin.

I weigh about sixty pounds. That is about the same as an eight-year-old human.

I am about four feet tall.

We live where it is very cold.
It is a place called Antarctica.
Antarctica is at the South Pole.

Galapagos penguin

Equator

Magellanic penguin

chinstrap penguin

Most penguin species live south of the **equator**.

Only the Galapagos penguin lives north of the equator.

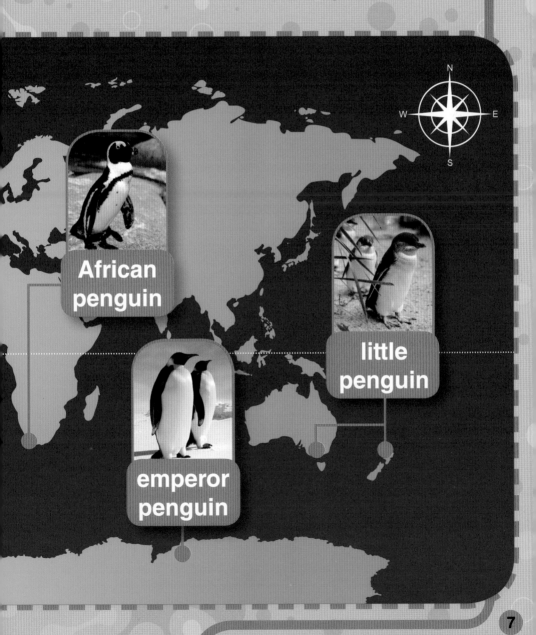

African penguin

little penguin

emperor penguin

Not all penguins live in cold places.

This penguin lives in Africa.

It makes a sound like a donkey.

The smallest penguin lives in Australia.

It is called a little penguin.

Little penguins are only about one foot tall.

They are blue and white.

Penguins are birds, but we cannot fly.

Half of our time is spent in the water.

We use our wings as flippers to swim.

Small penguins stay near the surface.

Large penguins like me can dive deep.

I can hold my breath for about twenty minutes!

Penguins are **carnivores**. We hunt small animals in the ocean.

squid

krill

My favorite food is fish. I also eat squid and tiny animals called krill.

Our mouths are spiny and rough inside.

Slippery fish cannot get away.

Penguins do not chew their food.

We swallow our food whole.

We are quick in the water.

But we are slower on land.

We have short legs and waddle as we walk.

We can move quicker if we hop.

Sometimes we slide on our bellies.

We use our feet to push us forward.

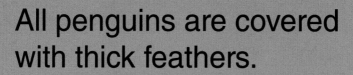

All penguins are covered with thick feathers.

Our feathers are very close together.

They trap air near our skin.

This keeps us warm in the water and on land.

Feathers wear out.
Penguins **molt** at least once a year.

During a molt, all of a penguin's feathers fall out.
New feathers replace the old ones.

My mate and I live in a **colony**.
A colony is a group of penguins.
Our colony sometimes has one thousand birds.
We all nest and hunt together.

This year my mate and I had a chick.

It was hard work!

I met my mate in April.

April is the beginning of winter in Antarctica.

It is a very cold time to lay an egg.

There is ice on the ground.

My mate laid her egg in May.
She carefully placed the egg
on my feet.

The egg could not touch the ice.
The chick inside would freeze.

I balanced the egg on my feet.
I tucked it under my tummy pouch.
The egg was safe and warm there.

Then my mate left to hunt for food.

I did not see her for two months.

But I was not alone.

All the dads in my colony stuck together.

We huddled close to stay warm in the wind.

We took turns being on the cold outside.

I protected the egg for sixty-four days.

I did not eat.

I made sure my egg stayed warm.

Then one day the egg hatched!

The chick still had to be kept warm. She stayed on my feet under my pouch.

I fed the chick a liquid from my throat.

Finally, the mother penguins returned.

Some walked over fifty miles back to the colony.

My mate called to me and I answered.

I was so happy to see her!

Then it was my turn to look for food.

While I was gone, my mate fed the chick.

She **regurgitated** food from her stomach.

The chick was always hungry!

We took turns caring for the chick.

She grew fast!

Now our chick huddles with her friends while we hunt.

This group of young penguins is called a **creche**.

I hear my chick calling.
It is my turn to feed her.
Thank you for visiting!

Glossary

carnivore: an animal that eats meat

colony: a group of animals living together

creche: a group of young animals that stay together for warmth

equator: an imaginary line around Earth that is halfway between the North and South Poles

molt: when feathers fall out to make room for new ones

regurgitate: to bring food up out of the stomach

species: a group of living things different from all other groups